HAPPY ENDING

David Rat

Published by Open Books 2012

Cover art "Addicted to creativity" by Danielle Kerr
Learn more about the artist at www.menitti.com

ISBN: 0615722881

ISBN-13: 978-0615722887

FOR JAMES

David Rat

CONTENTS

WHAT PEOPLE ARE SAYING ABOUT DAVID RAT, HAPPY ENDING AND RAT AT RAT R

"There are more fresh musical ideas on Rat At Rat R`s first album than one could absorb in an entire day of listening to hit radio." - Robert Palmer, N. Y. Times

"KING RAT!" - Katherine Ludwig, Paper Magazine

"WOW! KEITH MOON" - John McEnroe, tennis superstar

"A Fantastic Riot Boy! Trash the Senses!" - Thurston Moore, Sonic Youth

"Absolutely Beautiful ..but are you okay? I am worried about you." - Miss Sabrina, wife of rock legend Sky Saxon

"Dancing Master of the Ongoing" - Scott Wannberg, poet legend

"The way you feel about my Music is the Way I feel about your writing" - Miss Brittany, Alabama Shakes

"Hauntingly Beautiful" - Linda Tolbert, supermodel

"Keats is Alive and Well, Obviously" - Teri Louise Kelly, author-publisher, Blunt Trauma Press

"You are a gem Mr. Rat, Genius as usual!" - Beauregard Houston-Montgomery, East Village Eye

"You are going to Heaven, God told me so" - Verless Doran, author

"I Love You Daddy" - James Sidney Tritt

"Go listen to that Rat at Rat R record that came out in 1985, you'll hear stuff no one else was doing." - Glenn Branca, composer

"The soul that wrote this book is beyond the grime of winner or loser..amazing" - Bob Auclaire, artist-television personality

"Had to pick my heart up off the floor and put it back in my chest..Too close, too real" - Julie Dulak, animal rights activist and rescuer

"WOW!!!" - Lady Bunny, drag queen superstar

"Powerful! Will likely help a lot of people who are burdened with their own secrets." - Elizabeth Freund, Beautiful Day Media

"A Fine Writer" - Angela Bowie, author and architect of rock and roll

"Renews my faith that human beings really do need one another" - Cyndi Dawson, rockstar poet

"Thank you David." - Laura Kennedy, Bush Tetras

"So perfectly beautiful" - Dava She Wolf, rock and roll star

"Shows no fear, Sensitive and full of Hope" - Jim Fouratt, rock visionary and political activist

"Whitman, Thoreau, and Palahniuk all wept while i pulled myself closer to the page." - Sarah Free, artist

"The most ingenious, most beautiful, deepest thing I've ever seen put into print. I am in complete awe" - Jack Daniels Jr., author

"The second greatest living writer" - Kaplowitz, author

"I Hope they find you dead on the streets with your veins full of Smack" - My ex-wife

A NOTE FROM ANGIE

David,
I am very fond of you,
but this fixation with only
writing about drugs has to end. I am sick of it aren't you?
You know I care or I wouldn't bother to say anything...
start living and writing
start feeling life
before the sands have gone and trickled through your
clenched fists.......
love,
Angie

FORWARD
BY FIONA HELMSLEY

Most people have a dream epoch, a bygone era that they venerate and romanticize, thinking if only I'd been around for that. My pedestalled period on the space/time continuum is New York City in the mid 1970s and early '80s, my favorite city's last gasp for vibrant, inspired living on the cheap. One could still move to New York just to be an artist, not to just look like an artist while spending all of ones time working a shitty job just to make the rent.

Engendered by the cheap rents and lowered cost of living, New York City experienced a gritty, creative renaissance led by an underclass of young throwaways cut from the same angelic/demonic mold as Jean Genet and Arthur Rimbaud. Archetype artists like Richard Hell and Lydia Lunch sought reprieve from their damages onstage at clubs like CBGBs, Max's Kansas City and the Pyramid. Both were runaways to the city from screwed up homes.

Oscar Wilde famously said, "We are all in the gutter, but some of us are looking at the stars." In 1970s/'80s New York, a generation of impassioned street kids used artistic expression to lift their heads from the gutter and towards heaven.

Enter David Rat, a small town boy with the face of an

Adonis and big city rock n roll dreams. *Happy Ending* recounts David's early adulthood in late 1970s/ '80s New York. The drummer for seminal art noise band Rat At Rat R, David works the door at the infamous downtown Pyramid Club, juggles clingy girlfriends and looks forward to finally garnering his father's approval as mainstream success with his band beckons. The story-telling quality of David's poetry recounts the lyrical elegies of Lou Reed's "Walk on the Wild Side" and Iggy Pop's "Look Away." Doomed, tragic luminaries of the period like Greer Lankton and Ethyl Eichelberger provide the inspiration for some of David's best work. Once David becomes addicted to heroin, the names and wide-eyed descriptions of the era drop off, with testimonies to painful longing and the ritual redundancies of addiction taking their place.

I've always liked Angela Bowie, but I found her note to David that opens *Happy Ending* to be completely off the mark. In it, Angela flatters David but then asks when his "fixation" with writing about drugs will end. Writing about addiction when one has spent time counting lifelines from the inside of its clenched fist is not "fixation," it's *transcription*. Reducing the all-encompassing impact of addiction to some kind of fetish subject matter is not only smug, it completely nullifies the power of *Happy Ending*. It's the optimism despite the ugliness that makes *Happy Ending* so potent. Heroin robs David of his family and his rock n roll dreams, but he still eagerly reaches out for love, sees the beauty in the graying faces all around him and fights passionately for a better world for his beloved son. *Happy Ending* is about the resistance of the spirit to cynicism. It's also about the hopeful exorcism of ones demons with the pen.

David Rat came to New York City in the late 1970s to be an artist, and as *Happy Ending* attests, David still believes that art can set him free.

FROM THE AUTHOR

Writing *Happy Ending* was among the most miserable experiences of my life; I will never again put pen to paper to spew such maudlin emo-drive. From now on I will write only children's books. If you enjoy a good cry I suppose *Happy Ending* is a worthwhile read, but be sure to remove all sharp objects from the room and have access to a good therapist.

My story starts with a dream come true, progresses through its subsequent decline and ends with a big question mark. It follows me through jails, rehabs, rock and roll and park benches, and (I'm hoping) a little bit of hope, perhaps even redemption, someday...

The process of writing this book was painstaking, sometimes only a few pages a year. I had to be in a different state of mind entirely in order to let my guard down and be as honest as I could be. I'm not a devout minimalist but I did try to convey as much as I could in as few words as possible. I've done my best to "write the dangerous stuff" because most of this period of my life I had no dignity anyway, so it was easy not to care what anyone thought of me. It was a very different way of creating because rock and roll is all about appearing "cool", whereas my writing style may be brutal but is, by all accounts, honest.

Anyway, the hardest part was writing about the estrangement of my son. However, things are looking up; I have a new family and I am providing for and have a long distance relationship with my little boy. Also my new wife, step-daughter and animals bring me great joy. Life is actually good and getting better: I am a teacher now, and I am making a difference.

I am rescuing dogs again.

I am drug free...

The title of the book began as a play on words; "Happy Ending" as in "happy that life is ending", however it has apparently moved beyond the irony into a different meaning altogether.

Here is my story...

LETTER TO AN AIDS VICTIM
IN HEAVEN

The last time I saw you
on 13th and A
I wiped
the sweat
from your brow
and Lauren said,
"Wash your hands."

I just wanted
you to know
I dumped
that
stupid
bitch.

BORN TO USE

The disease crept in with the new dawn,
with a slap seemingly from God's hand.
I was awake...the smell of cat urine and lilac filled the air.
"I'm fucking sick," I groaned to no one.

With the reality of my 46 too-far-gone years I reached for
the wake up bag.
"Let me up, Monkey," I whispered to the old brown dog.
I wished I could do something more than make him
comfortable.
The infection had taken him over, still his heart filled his
eyes,
those big beautiful junkyard eyes that bleed brown sorrow,
enough beauty and sadness to drown the whole Human
Race
in a sick little dog's eyes....

In the kitchen I washed a blackened table spoon,
reached into my pocket for the glass rig
and nearly fell down the basement stairs.
As I reached the bottom I counted the hours in my head -
"8 to 9; 9 to 10; 10 to 11."

My dyslexia made me count this tedious routine a
thousand times a day.
I finally arrived at 1:00 pm, London time, and gently
opened the crystalline bag.

As always, I wondered what she was doing at that very
moment.
I filled the cloudy glass with water:
"Maybe lunch"...

The syringe shot a tiny stream into the silver spoon;
I cooked the brown powder and water till it bubbled.

I could feel her walking around like an amputated leg,
still itching 3,000 miles away.
I tied off my wrist with my belt and pumped my hand,
coaxing the nearly collapsed veins to the surface.

"Maybe she's thinking of me right now..."

I dug the needle into a spider vein and cocked back a little;
the blood and smack formed a holy union in the chamber.

"Maybe she's with him..."

I untied my wrist and pushed off,
and like a desperate police car prayer
I tried to tell myself
she didn't matter.
Then the rush....

Every junkie lives for those few seconds; the warm jets,
the sonic blanket,
the silent drowning of everything that means anything.
I fell back into the amber brick and pulled the gimmick
from my hand -
a quick rinse...

A little leftover metallic blood tasted like frost on the tip of
my tongue.

"She can't hurt you now," the heroin angels whispered.
Still, her jasmine hair
and suicide eyes
burned like oblivion.

Her ghost haunted the vacant day away.

I drank dollar store tea, rolled cigarettes and stroked the
dying animal's chin.

JADE

The only way I can speak of Jade
is to speak of her eyes.

I know, many tortured poets have gone on about a chick's
eyes:
"the doorway to a thousand churches"
"two infinite pools of light"
And other cornball musings...
But Jade had eyes you would
kill for...

Or die for!

Lose your sanity over...

They were HUGE,
and blue as the first night the world was born.

They were the color of Marilyn Monroe's car;
the color of Picasso's guitar.

Royal-baby-azure-colbalt-blue...
Blind-howlin'-Coltrane-chemical-timberwolf blue.

Her hair, however, was black as the winter sea;
as black as God's tears;
blacker than an overdose....

Needless to say, this combination was stunning.
Her eyes and hair and pale skin melded together (along
with a vicious pout)
into a spiritual tsunami...
And she lay wrapped in my dirty sheets
like a sleepy butterfly bruise....
My snow white, my wicked witch,
my fallen angel.

Jade didn't follow trends the other girls followed - she was
ashamed of her generation.
She could have been Keith Richard's wife, circa 1972,
with her bell-bottoms and corsets and Jackie O sunglasses.
She wanted nothing of zombie video games or ipods;
she wore dark black makeup,
no pink angora or lattes or TRL afternoons
hip hop dancing
with the Chosen Ones.
Instead she listened to Joni Mitchell and danced alone in
her room...
And Leonard Cohen and Eva Cassiday: she read Harper
Lee and Sylvia Plath.
And she could sing! Jade could sing...
But I can't write much about that now,
not without opening my veins on this keyboard,
because when she sang to me I was the only man on earth.
Her voice was angel heroin on high.
And that's all you need to know...
Except,
I guess you can tell,
I really loved her.
She was my English rose,

my falling star.
But to her
I'm just a
junkie...

With ghosts
in his eyes,

Across
the ocean....

MONKEY

Huddled against me,
too mean to love anyone else,
thrown away and beaten -
you can't blame us
for hating you.

WAR

I've known functioning alcoholics:
the single dad who drinks himself into a stupor
with a six pack or two after work...

And there are functioning potheads:
blazing up out behind
their minimum wage prisons at lunch break...

Even functioning cocaine addicts
that can do an 8-ball,
drink away the depression
and be at the office
bleary eyed and penniless
the very next day...
But there is no such thing
(I repeat)
no such thing
as a functioning heroin addict.
Heroin is the mafia queen bitch of all drugs;
in other words, once you're in, you ain't getting out.

Because...

She is the sun and the moon,
your life, your heart, your soul;
everything belongs to her.
Yes, people have been known to "recover"...
I did.
I went to Narcotics Anonymous meetings in New York,
Los Angeles...
Sometimes managing to put six months together here, a
year there...
I was even clean for four years once in New York,
signed to a major record label, living with the teen Euro-
trash model,
or the trust fund cookie of the month...
My bandmates were the darlings of the press.
I took a *New York Times* article
home for my grandmother to read.
I became friends with artists
I'd idolized as a child,
opened for Ginsberg
in Thompkins Square.

My father
got to see me
play on network television once
(the yardstick by which artistic merit
is measured in rural America).
But in the end
she never let go of my hand,
and for that reason alone
she was better than any woman.
Better than any friend
or family member.

She was true love, angel smack,
goddess of everything,
the warm womb.

Happy Ending

Monkey was the only constant in my life,
the one little promise I kept.
Which is a rare and wondrous thing
when coming from a junkie.
I shoplifted dog food; I painted the vet's office:
in return I got the kind of devotion no human being has
ever aspired to.

But now with one love,
a black bird across
a black ocean...

And one love dying
in my arms a little more
each night...
Neither gods nor man
will stop me.

NEWARK

"Where does the flight from London come in?"
I was shaking like a leaf;
it had been seven months
since I'd met her online.

During those seven months I'd managed to go from a high
school
friend's couch, strung out,
with 100 milligrams of methadone
to six months clean, a little Korean car and a rented house
in a white trash town.

Nestled into gray Pennsylvania mountains,
it wasn't exactly the kind of place I'd envisioned for us.

A coal mining town,
after the mines had closed...
A black and blue toothache of a bedroom community
with a reputation for hillbillies and hard drugs.
I hooked up with the local recovery folks,
and didn't go out of my way to meet anyone.

23

This fucking town was razor sad.

But our house was clean and warm,
and it was there that I curled up with Monkey in my arms
at night,
both of us dreaming of our new mama.

Spending countless hours on MSN...
Then the phone...then the webcam...
there were poems...
and promises,
sad sadistic lovemaking,
and emptiness,
but...
There was a reason;
Now I had a reason.
And, yes, she was decades younger...
And, yes, I had met her on the Internet...
And, yes, most of you
would shake your heads and disapprove...
As everyone did when I told them about her.

And yet, we all have our preferences...
And at the very least,
unlike heroin,
she was legal.
People were coming off the plane now.
I looked like Stevie Nicks
in my gypsy scarf and long '70s-style coat.
I hid behind a pole as an eternity ended,
and she walked into the reception.

I was fucking freaked!
There is no feeling as intense and terrifying
as meeting someone for the first time;
someone you've been desperately in love with
for months.

But there she was, walking toward me,
dressed in a short black skirt
and velvet boots;
my little boho-goth chick
looking like Euro-trash royalty
gone wrong.
Our eyes met and the world came to a halt.
I was lost in electric blue,
ivory white skin
and vicious pink lips.
I bit them gently and brushed my fingertips
against the side of her face,
and we fell, like an ocean on fire,
everything crashing down around us.
The needles and the razorblades,
the suicide notes drenched
with one million tears,
the park benches,
and the rehabs,
prison cells
and abortions:
All gone,
Burnt down,
Sent to me,

By a little girl's smile.

THE SADDEST WORDS EVER WRITTEN

Your bumper sticker reads:
"God bless America"
but says nothing
about the rest of us...

MISS ANTHROPY

I know you don't "know" me;
but you do!
You walk by us everyday,
by the hundreds in a month's time,
We are the losers, the shot out, the fucked up...
Strung out on pills or wine or cutting ourselves with
razorblades;
a few too many three martini lunches,
or one too many lost friends or broken hearts:
and,
we go down:
And,
We stay there...

Ghosts walking around dead,
too fragile for this world.

Let's face it;
it's a horrible mistake:
gods forbid there is ever another Human Race:
we are the blood-thirstiest,
dirtiest and most destructive

soul-less machine
to ever grace any planet in the universe.

And what's worse is that
Everything we believe is wrong!

And, on top of that,
we're arrogant.

Thinking we know anything (with 90% of our brain
undeveloped),
we are a blip on the radar, an experiment gone wrong,
a piece of time between Ice Ages.
too small to have a name.

It's all too stupid; I mean, Jesus, Jehovah, Allah, whatever...

Idiot American Puritans were shocked
when John Lennon said he was more popular than Jesus
Christ:
He *was* Jesus Christ.

As was Ghandi...
As was Martin Luther King...
These people tried,
they tried,
they tried so desperately to teach us
to love one another....
And we killed them.

We couldn't grasp the concept,
because loving your fellow man
means loving them more than money;
and very few people
love very few people
more than that.
Hooray for capitalism!

Hooray for America!

But it's time to understand
that when you have "winners",
you must also have losers.

And we aren't going away.

David Rat

GOING OUT

"Fucking hell this is good sm................," I said.
And in that fleeting instant,
everything was nothing.

She stood over me screaming,
pulling the gimmick from my arm,
tearing the shoelace from my wrist.
She was barely eighteen, from Taiwan and
ill prepared to cope with a junkie boyfriend
whose lips were turning blue.

My nephew Chad, and my running partner Matt
came from the next room.
Chad started CPR
as Matt ground his knuckles into my chest.

Later, sitting in rehab,
I was actually pissed at the poor guy
for the bruises he'd made while saving my life.

They flushed all the drugs and called 911.
I woke up in the ambulance with EMT's

screaming my name.

Motherfuckers had shot me up with Narcan.
Funny thing is,
Narcan is supposed to put you into immediate withdrawl,
but as I rode to the hospital I was still high.

I was clinically dead for a few minutes.

And it wasn't at all like I thought it would be...
There was nothing - not a fucking thing!
No angels. No trumpets. No white light at the end of the
tunnel.
Just the thick black swamp of oblivion.
I met Matt at a record store.
He was my age,
An $80,000-a-year health insurance executive
with a wife/car/house.
He wore suits to work.
We were the oddest couple.
Matt's dead.
He got busted and rolled over
on Kojak (the wrong guy)
and ended up with a hot shot.
He wasn't even a banger.
The smack they gave him was pure;
he snorted it and nodded out behind the wheel on
Interstate #81.
I was in L.A. when I got the call from his wife.

In the junkie business
you get used to your friends dying after awhile,
but I had given Matt his first fix; I felt responsible,
and according to his wife I was!
Chad was one of the few human beings
I have ever felt true love from.
He was my first (drunk and abusive) wife's nephew.

Happy Ending

He was five when I met him,
a blonde haired, blue eyed cherub of a little boy from a
broken home.

In my fumbling way, I tried to be a father figure.

He really didn't have much in the way of a male role model

whichever gold-chain-wearing coke freak was around that
week.
So I suppose I was an improvement.

He had an incredible gift for all things artful;
he drew me pictures of rock stars with his crayons.
He did little performances for me in my living room.

"Look, Uncle David, I'm an ice cube melting!"
Curled up into a square, he slowly dripped
into a cherub tow head puddle on the floor.

Never has such a little bit of kindness come back
to any human being in such a magnificent way!
It was Chad that I called from Queens General
(psychiatric evaluation)
for help.
I was crumbling and scared,
dressed in blue slippers,
at the end of my run.

But it's funny, you know.
When you get to the end of it all,
it's calm:
the defeat of the jail cell,
or rehab,
or halfway house...

It's peaceful

when you hang your head in shame
and realize you have to live again.

He sent me a bus ticket and we stayed together
in the basement of the tattoo parlor where he worked for
years.
A truly golden soul, Chad...
He never gave up on me;
there are such people in the world -
at least one.
The police came to the hospital and questioned me.
I had copped out of their jurisdiction so they carted me off
to rehab.
Two weeks for the county to decide I wasn't worth
the $1,000-dollars-a-day it would cost to get me clean.
And I came home to Chad...

She was waiting,
a smile on her face.
A few weeks later her parents
took her back to Taiwan
(to get her away from me)
and stranded her there without her passport.
She was five months pregnant with my child
when she finally returned.
Her brothers threw her in a car
and drove her across State lines,
where it was legal to have a late term abortion.
When I finally saw her months later
I put my head on her lap
and sobbed in front
of a room full
of strangers.

WE DID IT TO OURSELVES

I'm walking around dead,
twenty years of bashing my veins,
red stains in the bathroom sink...

Jails
Rehabs
Park benches
Mom...
Everyone
can drag me out
in the middle of ground zero,
put out my eyes
with your little American flags,
fly on your Japanese cars...

I don't give a fuck;
I'll say it!

David Rat

KOJAK

I met him when I was nineteen.
I had a small part in a Sam Shepard play,
and he played the lead.
In the midst of a forced "financial" methadone detox,
I found him in the parking lot of the clinic.

A financial detox is when you can't pay your bill and they
take you down 10 mgs a day.
It's fast and furious, and when you reach the end you are
fucked.
Ripped apart like a rag doll, sucked null, void and dry.
All for the want of ninety dollars.

A small but often impossible price to pay
for the bright warm love now leaving your cells,
desperate and dying of pink thirst.
The place was snuggled right between the main road and
the hill
(every dope neighborhood in Pennsylvania is called "the
hill")
In Pittsburgh I spent nine days dope-sick in the arms of a

David Rat

West Virginia stripper
because we were white and couldn't go on "the hill".
Kojak and his wife Mary Ann had forty cats.
They were cold and heartless when it came to dope
business.

They never turned a cat away;
they were the neighborhood drop-off for unwanted litters
or abandoned, battle scarred veterans with missing eyes
and shredded ears...
Animals thrown away by people more heartless than even
us.
Somehow they managed to feed their animals,
support their habit
and keep from being evicted.
Nearly functional junkies with a sliver of a soul, left
behind.
She had a beautiful garden
filled with flowers and rusty garbage and feral cats staring
like they knew something
about you that
you didn't.
The ritual went as follows: I'd call them first, then make
the twenty minute drive,
hand Kojak the money, and he'd go cop for us.
It took him anywhere from ten minutes to a few hours if it
was hot,
but he always came through.
Then to the upstairs bathroom I went,
where I rummaged through the plastic bag of dirty needles,
searching for one that was bleach worthy.

Often the syringes were so old that the rubber tip would
separate from the plunger...
in which case I would grease them with a bit of Vaseline
and a prayer.
I hated bleaching - desperate and kicking -

(taking time to run bleach through the gimmick seemed
like an eternity)
but Kojak insisted (three times always, then three rinses);
the old junkie with the heart of a used car dealer
probably saved my life a thousand times.
Once we were all high, business went out the window.
We laughed and chain smoked: once in a while we had
money for food.
Mary Ann made dinner,
and we'd sit back to watch the black and white movies on
their pirated cable.
Hepburn and heroin; sugary tea and dusty stained
furniture;
yellow eyes drooling; ferocious purring; raggedy dog at my
feet:
the best and worst times of my life.
He was completely bald since a young age, hence the name
Kojak.
She was slightly retarded, or learning disabled,
or maybe just brain damaged from ten bags of heroin a
day.
But her mannerisms exhibited some kind of twisted
poetry.
She formed slow sentences with a Lydia Lunch whine,
childlike,
calculating.

She worked relentlessly in the garden, staying high, caring
for the cats.
She slobbered mutant baby talk to them in the same sweet
voice
that ordered the hot shot for Trent,
leaving my friend a ghost on the highway,
lifeless,
junkie-blue,
and unable to testify
against us.

David Rat

POPPIES

Will it be
you and me?
Or
another
fucking
cup
of
tea?

David Rat

DOWN

At one point my partners were named
Larry and Moe...
Seriously!

I was the third stooge in a dirty town with a blackened
steak in my heart.
Moe was an old man who was the one friend that every
junkie should have.
He was DIABETIC -
that meant CLEAN NEEDLES for life!

Moe was the original fuck-up, real old-school junkie trash,
scrawny with greased back hair and amber tinted '70s
sunglasses.
He also had a car...
A diabetic with a car - my new best friend.

The car was a decrepit Datsun.
I remember we had to lift the hood
and jiggle the battery cable before we split.
Once we were out trying to score and a car was following

us around.
We were sure it was the cops.
We were so paranoid we called the dealer and moved our
spot in order to lose them.
When the vehicle pulled up to the new location, we
completely freaked out.
We lifted the hood of the car to fix the cable,
then piled in the back,
and Moe said: "This ain't no getaway car."

Soon we realized that the "police" were actually other
customers.
Moe's apartment was a great place to hang out and get
high.
It had a crusty loveliness, all gray and green, institutional.
With a spare bedroom and a chemi-mechanical array of
goodies:
sterile, shiny, plastic, perfect new syringes (some were even
made of glass).
These were the interferon needles
(like chemo for Hep C victims).

.

Poor Moe had to shoot himself in the stomach once a
week
with this horrible drug that made him sick as fuck.
I answered the phone one morning, sick with no wake up,
and it was Moe wanting to know if I needed anything.

This meant I had to buy him a bag.
But to me it was just cheap insurance.
I hated copping.

So the day started out with Moe coming to pick up money.
He took off for Alison Hill.
A few minutes after he'd left
I got another call from my probation officer.
Her name was Kerry; she was hardcore.

We had an odd relationship.
I think she saw something in me worth saving.
She told me I needed to take a urine test at the local police
station.

My heart sank as I thought about the dope
that Moe would be returning with shortly.
When he got back and I told him he said,
in his gravelly Dutch Cleanser voice,
"You can't fix man, you can't fix.
Go take your test,
get it over with,
come back and get off."
So off I went to the Camp Hill police department.
I laughed and joked with the officer on duty;
I had been through this before.
As I finished I said, "Have a nice night."

He said, "Hold on a minute, I have some bad news.
Your last two tests came up hot.
Stand up, take everything out of your pockets.
You're going to prison tonight."

Calm terror - thirsty cells
down, down,
way on down...

I put my hands behind my back
and walked to a tiny holding cell
with shackles on my legs.
Two bags of smack screamed
from my dresser drawer.

David Rat

WITCH TRIAL

You were still pretty
when I burned your photograph.
Your skin became marble,
blue eyes
became white.
These diamonds
at the bottom
of a black creek now,
a promise
to fishes
so they
can
know
love.

David Rat

C-BLOCK

I haven't written all that much about kicking,
probably because it's so horrible a fate
to even think about it.

I must have kicked dope fifty times.
And kicking in jail?
A hell of my own making!

Lying on the concrete floor under my bunk
to try to hide from the jagged shards of light
tearing me apart...
At one with the dust bunnies and the filth
from the other poor souls before me.

Miserable ghosts with anguish thick as fog...
Puking, shaking, tremors; too hot, too cold,
can't sleep, moaning, wrapped in those green wool
blankets,
thinking about the two bags in my dresser at home.
Razorblades in my stomach, gagging. Begging, crying.
Walking back and forth,

endlessly.

Trying so desperately
just to sleep.

But sleep never comes.
Awake for twenty-three days,
on suicide-watch,
not even fifteen minutes of sleep,
you meet a side of yourself you never knew,
one you never thought possible.
After twenty days awake,
living dead...
I thought I was Keith Richards
leaning on the bar with a
crystal red wine glass,
nodding and scratching my face,
mumbling ethereal cigarette poetry.
But for every twelve hours spent
fading into blurry stars on the walls
of a warm wet womb
there is a debt to be paid,
and this was it!

THE PLACE WHERE DREAMS GO TO DIE

me....

David Rat

GEN-POP

In my prison cell I lay on the stained mattress
and felt my central nervous system
tingle and crack.

Breaking through the black ice
in which I had entombed the splinters of my heart
my mind began to sputter, ignite and spark
like a greasy old muscle car engine.
Fueled by food and sleep
in this hillbilly county jail
I finally begin to feel free.
This is no ordinary lock-up:
minimum security, edible food, good library,
no rapists in the shower.
The guards turn a blind eye when we
beat the fuck out of the child molesters.
When my foot bloodied the face of a soulless bastard
doing time for abusing his nine-year-old son,
I was filled with a loving vengeance,
closer to the gods than I had ever felt before.
I dreamt of a new me,

an avenging angel with hate and light streaming
from every meridian.
An ocean of blood,
orange electric love
for every single lost, forgotten
and wounded living thing.
I made friends with the rest of these sad but colorful
characters.
We were stranded together on this acid-washed cruise ship
that knew no harbor.
In church the preacher told me that
"God builds armies from prison."
In Narcotics Anonymous
I was told that I was
"one of the chosen ones".
A gasoline soaked rag
pulled from the world's rubbish.
A trashcan dream,
washed clean in
God's laundromat.

JAMES, I WROTE THIS FOR YOU

Today
at Narcotics Anonymous
someone said
they heard
a glimmer of hope
in my voice...

That's what
you sound like.

David Rat

THIS IS WHY…

the Whites hate the Blacks
the light skinned Blacks hate the dark skinned Blacks
the Indians hate the Pakistani's
the British hate the Irish
the southern Irish hate the northern Irish
the light skinned Indians hate the dark skinned Indians
the Christians hate the Muslims
the Jews hate the Arabs
the Republicans hate the Democrats
the north of Italy hates the Sicilians
the Scots hate the Brits
the Catholics hate the Protestants
the homophobes hate the gays
New Zealand hates the Aussies
the neo-cons hate the liberals
the mods hate the rockers
the jocks hate the heads
the metal kids hate the emos
the chavs hate the goths
the French hate Americans
the North Koreans hate the South Koreans

the junkies hate the coke freaks
the Mormons hate love
the socialists hate the capitalists
the artists hate the yuppies
the Bloods hate the Crips
the vegans hate the hunters
the fat hate the thin
the mainstream hates the alternative
the Iraqi's hate the Iranians
the Hell's Angels hate the pagans
Idaho hates Californians
the yankees hate the rebels
the Chinese hate the Tibetians
the Californians hate the Armenians
the English hate the French
the hippies hate the establishment
the Texans hate the Mexicans
the meth-heads hate the crack-heads
the Methodists hate the Baptists
Afghanistan hates Russians
the clinically depressed hate themselves
the ranchers hate the wolves
the pro-life hate the pro-choice
Los Angeles hates New York
the Native Americans hate the white man
the bikers hate the cages
the Satanists hate the Christians
the rappers hate each other
the old hate the young
the poor hate the rich
the east hates the west
the dead hate the living
God hates America
America hates everyone

I'm cooking up.

VENGEANCE FOR VENGEANCE

I dream of gathering dead Islamic children
in a wheelbarrow,
infant blood thick
like chocolate over
coffee ice cream.
I wheel them center stage
at Madison Square Garden
with Bill and Hillary,
Richard Gere, Susan Sarandon...
Me dumping dead kids out
in the white hot spotlight
and stepping up to the mike
in front of thousands
of fat, drunken fireman and cops.

In my dreams
I whisper,
"Feel better?"

David Rat

BAG AND BAGGAGE

If I could have smoked in prison
I'd still be there.
I walked out front and lit up furiously.
The cigarette tasted like dizzy champagne;
black pink poison, gray wisps
of frozen breath...
I thought about the guns
I had stolen from my father,
sold to a smack dealer
named Angel
for China White salvation.
The fearless empty spaces
gave way to
acid rain.
These desperate dope-sick weapons
I had put on the street
could have been used
to kill something beautiful.
Maybe children...
My reflection disappeared
in the bail-bondsman's windshield,
and I knew I was
too far gone.

David Rat

SURVIVEICIDE

I lit a Marlboro
in the ambulance
with no bright light
to float toward.

David Rat

OH CANADA

I fucking love Canada.
I love the beer and jelly doughnut culture,
I love Bob and Doug McKenzie,
I love that in the '80s
I walked into a Canadian McDonalds,
ordered a Coke, handed them twenty bucks USD,
and they gave me the Coke and twenty-three dollars
Canadian.
The first tour I did in the Great White North with Rat At
Rat R
was supporting a Candian hardcore band called "dead
brain cells".
The drummer was a lovely and kind knucklehead named
Jeff (RIP).
He lined up chicks, dope dinners and a week's worth of
shows
in and around Montreal.
I was happy to leave New York for a few days.
My life had become complex due to a girl from
my hometown who (like a fool) followed me to NYC.
She was sweet and kind, yes,

67

but I had begun dating Lene,
the highest paid model in the U.K. at the time,
so I kissed Pennsylvania girl goodbye.
I remember her saying,

"Have a really good time!"

VCRs were a miraculous thing back then.
They had become affordable only months earlier,
and we all went out and bought shiny new beta machines
for a hundred bucks.
We went to Tower Records (where I worked for a time)
and rented movies daily.
We stayed up late making copy after copy,
building huge video libraries.
What a revelation this was!
We could program our own televisions - amazing!
When I see twelve-year-olds today,
with the Internet on their cell phones,
I just shake my head.

Anyway, one of our favorite films was *Strange Brew*.
We became obsessed with Canada.
We started saying "Eh" after every sentence,
quoting the film at nearly every juncture of our daily lives.

Fifteen minutes before we crossed the border
we thought we'd better ditch the drugs.
I remember my mother had packed some snacks
and (notorious speed freak that she was)
I thought I'd better have a look.

Opening some stale X-mas cookies she had thrown in
I found a little bag of a hundred or so black beauties
(remember those?):
Thanks, Mom, for the dope,
and the almost eight years in a Canadian prison.

We stopped and I left the pills in a phone booth
for some other poor fuck-up to happen upon
(couldn't waste Mom's drugs).

When we reached the border we attracted a bit of
attention.
Sonda and I looked like some rock and roll-street-urchin-
Hell's Angels.
Victor, in long black coat and hair,
with a metal lunchbox full of little sci-fi figurines...

But Jeff had hooked us up with a letter from a Canadian
recording studio
stating that we were on our way to work there.
Customs approved of that cause -
we were coming to Canada to spend money rather than
earn it,
and they finally waved us through.

At the first show I was given twenty drink tickets;
alcohol was never my fix, but beer was
the cornerstone of Canadian culture.
People stood in lines around the block to buy beer,
just like we stood in line for Bruce Springsteen tickets.
So I surveyed the girls in line, chose the hottest one
and offered her the tickets.
Beer must truly be the key to a Canadian's heart,
because she rarely left my side the rest of the week.
She spoke French,Iitalian and Spanish,
but very little English.

During sound check we were talking our usual strange-
brew language:
"Plug that in over here, eh?" "You hoser!" etc.
I noticed that the audience that was let in early began to
look at us with disdain;
they thought we were making fun of them.

David Rat

Little did they know we were paying homage
to our beloved Canada.

Upon returning to Manhattan
I walked into the apartment I shared with
"Pennsylvania chick"
to find it cleaned out
(even my precious VCR was gone);
she had split to marry an engineer,
leaving Victor and I to stand there
scratching our heads.

I guess she got tired of me dogging her.

I squatted in her abandoned apartment for another six
months,
turning it over to some homeless Rastafarians
when I left to be with Lene.

Last I heard,
they had converted her entire bathroom
into one huge bong!

UNREQUITED

At least I am man enough
to wake up every morning,
breathe in and out
and smile at old people...

Oblivion,
a phone call away.

David Rat

JAMES

I don't want to write anymore.
All I seem to be able to do is
make you cry.
I want you to smile.

It's been five long weeks
since my last hateful fix.

Tired of hurting myself;
tired of hurting my son.

I don't want him
to grow up a junkie.

Or a poet.

Or, God forbid,
a rock and roller.

Maybe a CPA,
like his godmother,

David Rat

in khaki and Navy
imported granite,
peaceful stainless steel appliances,
dark wood cabinetry.

Maybe he'll love jazz.

The occasional white wine
(with dinner).

Maybe he'll close his eyes
on crisp cold autumn evenings,
and dream a different dream.

Surrounded by laughing children
and redemption dogs.
A good woman by his side.

With a smile like my Mother's,
strong and guarded,
capable.

Like my Daddy.
No demons,
no self destruction,
no diseased bleeding heart
or eternally open wound.

Maybe he'll be smart,
like his mama,
and have the sense to leave.

Maybe he'll hate me,
and all that I am

I can only hope.

GREER

The East Village early '80s:
our fourteen square blocks
of pure boho glory!
We sold our televisions for drug money
and sat on blurry stoops
seceding from the
United Hate of America.
Fed by the Hare Krishna's,
we smoked dope on the street
and bathed in tenement kitchens
filled with garbage and glitter.
A few months off the bus
from Pennsylvania farmlands,
I met her at Civilian Warfare,
a gallery owned by
another oh-so-beautiful dead friend,
Dean Sarvard.
My price of freedom was
a graveyard for a rolodex,
and sometimes survival seems
like my only friend left alive.

She wasn't my type at all;
tall blonde, forlorn hazel eyes,
legs like a newborn colt.
We got high
and paraded around the city together,
arm in arm,
like ragged ghosts.
Lunch at Cafe Orlin,
then a dinner party
on Central Park West,
a cast of luminaries in attendance.
Lydia was there with Rollins,
Sonic Youth, Swans, Live Skull, etc.
Henry had somehow procured new
Charles Manson recordings.
Amid schmoozing,
and bites of tortellini,
a woman remarked,
"You have such a lovely deep voice, Greer."

When I walked into her apartment
it was like Disney on purple mescaline,
life-size horrific dolls
modeled after Herself,
Terri Toye, Divine and Candy Darling,
ripped apart, stitched up,
strewn everywhere.
A ballerina hacked in half was
outdone only by a doll on her deathbed,
littered with empty pill bottles.

Staring at gold stars
painted on the ceiling...
Every idiot in the Village
with a can of spray paint
was a "visual artist".

Happy Ending

But Greer was for real;
her work was truly visceral,
like surgery without anesthesia.
She had been part of Warhol's factory
and knew simply everyone;
she had shown at the Whitney
and worked for Jim Henson,
actually applying yellow feathers
to the very first Big Bird costume.

A little cocaine,
one soul wrenching,
red wine kiss...

And I was hopelessly searching
for something eloquent to say:
"You must have been a really pretty little girl,"
I stammered clumsily.

"Um, no,
I was a really confused,
fucked up little boy,"
she (he) replied softly.
Granted, those were crazy
life changing months,
but where I'd come from
we didn't even have Chinese food!

let alone
beautiful
post-op
transsexual
art superstar
chicks...

In the pit of my stomach
my head exploded,

but outwardly I kept my cool
remembering that my idol, Lou Reed,
had supposedly married a transsexual.

I lit two Marlboros,
and we talked...

"Greg" was the effeminate son
of a Presbyterian minister from Illinois,
bullied, beaten and teased,
relentlessly.

He retreated into a world of
solace and doll making.
At twenty-one years old,
with financial help from his father's church,
Greg became Greer...

So I did what any red blooded
American farm boy would do:
I kept seeing her.
Aside from kissing and hand holding
we never had much of a physical relationship.
But I loved being with her:
we were wild
we were beautiful
we were damned!
In 1996, after desperately trying
to starve herself to death,
Greer finally overdosed
and faded away from me
under a deep blue ceiling
painted with gold-colored stars.

SLUGGO'S GALLERY

Rat At Rat R was a family - we truly were. I know all bands would like to think this, and in a way they would be right. When you're in a band with someone it's exactly like being married to them: you work together, play together, sleep together, suffer together, give birth together and all (and I do mean all!) that that entails.

I met John when we were five years old. It was my fifth birthday actually. We lived in a tiny village called Shepherdstown, population 300ish. We had a Methodist church, huge hills for sledding and an old hotel on a hilltop that had the only soda machine for thirty miles.

I'm not going to lie: John and I had great childhoods. We had cherry trees to climb, fresh grapes on the vine; we pulled carrots out of the ground, washed them off with the garden hose and ate them raw. We skated on frozen ponds, climbed through lime green quarries and fell asleep knowing that if we were ever in trouble we could knock on any door in our town and everything would be ok.

We saw Victor's band at an outdoor gig in the cultural abyss that was home (it was very rare at that time for a band to have any original songs, but their entire set was original). Amazing! John and I had recently turned our attentions from King Crimson and Yes to Television and Roxy music, and our young impressionable minds were blown.

Victor was brilliant, tall and rock star thin with long black hair like a big Bowie-esque country boy with a huge safety pin on his belt loop. So the legend goes that John was working at Howard Johnson's and Victor just happened in. A week later we were sitting - the three of us - in Victor's mom's basement surrounded by his paintings and sculptures, which were just ridiculously cool, especially to a seventeen-year-old farm boy drummer (Yours truly)! Mother Mary gazed into a silver hand mirror reflecting a stuffed rat whose insides were replaced with mechanical parts (entitled, "A Gift for Rose"). And my favorite: a young girl in a graduation cap and gown with a gun to her head. I remember asking what the painting was about. "Suicide," Victor answered. "We all commit suicide at different times in our lives," he said.

I remember him unleashing Holy Grail after Holy Grail upon us, from Cockney Rebel to Eno to Ultravox. He quickly became more of a mentor than a band mate.

Sonda was Victor's girlfriend and a real big sister to me. To this day she is the classiest woman I have ever met. Everything I know of style and grace I learned from Sonda, a gloriously beautiful mix of northern Italian and blond Scandinavian perfection. She smoked peacock-colored cocktail cigarettes from a bone cigarette holder. Nico in a raggedy motorcycle vest, she sparkled, throbbed and oozed behind her gold-top Gibson. Breathtaking!

So like any family we did stuff together.

I forget now whose idea it was to drop acid and go to Rock-a-way Beach. There is nothing funnier than a New York City no-wave redneck rock and roll band dressed up for the beach on a purple mescaline morning. Black cut-offs, muscle shirts, tube socks and Venus Flytrap sunglasses, we looked hysterical. In my drummer-like tank top and shorts I was quickly dubbed "Sluggo".

About the time we hit Rock-a-way the acid started to kick in: the waves became fused with bright fairy-light, the sun beat down like Thor's hammer. I remember us sitting there giggling like schoolgirls as everything became *MAAZING!*

Soon I was doing crazy little sculptures in the sand with shells, sticks and seaweed, much to everyone's amusement.

"Hey! Look at Sluggo; he's an *arteest! It's SLUGGO'S GALLERY!*"

We all laughed that crazy, core-shaking Lysergic laugh, the laugh you think will never stop. After that, all I remember is sitting in a trance in front of the dirty New York ocean listening to the sound of my sizzling skin, hypnotized by seagulls.

On the train back to Manhattan reality crept in and I realized how badly burned I was. I swear people were pointing and laughing as we slunk through the lower east side avoiding friends and fans to finally reach home and lick our wounds.

"Sluggo" never did open his art gallery, but when I think of that day I have to smile. I really miss my family.

Sonda is now an art director living in Virginia and has re-designed both the Village Voice and L.A. Weekly. She is married to a lovely Native American man and loves her Yorkies. I swear she must drink blood, because she is still as stunning as she ever was!

John gave me a CD once and said, "This is wood flute; this is for your kidneys..."

Victor lives with a lovely woman on Long Island and is still immersed in everything artistic.

And me? I am a cowboy poet in New Mexico with dogs, chickens, hummingbirds and late night train whistles...

watching
icy blue stars
fill the light sweet air.

David Rat

ETHYL

She slit her wrists
the night
of her
diagnosis.

Murdered
by hateful
ignorance,
she did a
children's show.
I loved him so;
so tired of hope.

David Rat

CHICK VEINS

Truth is
I was the most pathetic white boy junkie on the planet.
Hated copping; always paid someone to do it.
Cheap insurance...
Let them rot and kick in jail.

I was a machine
But...
it was ok.

I didn't have to hurt;
I didn't have to cry;
I didn't have to miss you;
I didn't have to love.

I didn't have to feel
that salty dead black sea
of nothingness,

that gnawing aching ripped up gash in my chest
where my child last laid his head.

(How could I have known it was the last time?)

I was cursed with fucking chick veins,
deep-set, thin and easily collapsed;
pitted, hard to hit.

So I got off in my hand...
No way to hide the tracks.
I wore them proudly anyway,
my message to the world.

Here is a broken man,
a man you threw away,
a man who will not participate
in this beautiful world
where a child starves to death
every five seconds...

1.
2.
3.
4.
5.

With swollen bellies
and green teeth
from fathers trying to
feed them grass
to keep them alive...

So fuck you!
The world needs losers
so others can win.

Sad clowns,
golden glittering train wrecks.

Beautiful disasters....

You need me to remind you
that things could always be worse.

David Rat

STEPHEN

I was nine years old,
sent to my grandmother's hairdresser for a "trim".
Even at nine I didn't want my hair cut,
but he had a little black poodle
that I loved.
The dog jumped into my lap
as I sat in the salon chair.
As the creep started to pet the dog,
his hand slipped between my legs.
He began to fondle me.
My entire life changed.
I told my father what had happened.

"Really?" was his only reply.
Not another word was spoken about the incident.
It was then that I truly understood
I was alone in this world,
worthless,
unwanted,
trash.
Sitting here today,

digging in my arm for a fresh vein,
I am hoping his death is as slow and miserable as mine.
Stephen was a violinist.
At seventeen he could play Paganini
with his eyes closed.
He was beautiful;
he was art.

The sound of his violin came straight from heaven
and spiraled deep into my stomach,
where it still lives to this day.
My favorite story about Stephen
was when he and John (my best friend and guitarist)
took a bunch of windowpane acid and split,
hitchhiking down Route #15 towards California.
When the cops rolled up and asked for I.D.,
Stephen refused.

As John handed his driver's license to the officer,
Stephen grabbed it,
shoved it into his mouth
and ate it.
How could you not love such a man?
He began to behave more erratically;
one day he called a band meeting
and smashed his violin in front of us.
"I'm Free!" he exclaimed.
When I visited him in the State hospital
he talked of being molested by the orderlies.

I felt sick in my stomach,
flashing back to my own ordeal.
"What are we going to do about this?" I asked him.
"Nothing."
"Why?"
"I'm used to it."
"What do you mean?"

Happy Ending

"My father."

Stephen's father was an evangelical Christian.
They found his body in Yellow Breeches Creek.
My childhood friend had drowned himself.

I wondered if he felt the same as I
while the black creek water filled his lungs.
The self hatred;
the worthlessness;
the anger,
abandonment,
the guilt...
Thrown away by the world,
unwanted,
trash.
When I visit the cemetery
I want to reach down through
that gray graveyard dirt;
I want to hold his hand,
I want to hold him in my arms.
I just want to tell him,

"It's ok;
It's ok;
It's ok."

It's not ok...

David Rat

THE GIFT

Deep breaths,
sad smiles,
ice on tree branches.

Broken wings,
blue silk,
deafening snow.

Tears cried from burning clouds,
flowers made of mirrored trash.

Still I sleep
in this emptiness
I have laid
at your feet.

David Rat

GO BACK TO NEW JERSEY

I found refuge
in the worst place
you could ever put
a New Yorker.
You guessed it:
fucking New Jersey!
I had been such an arrogant prick
to the poor bridge and tunnel kids
I turned away from the door
of the Pyramid Club.
I think I even told a few of them to
"Go back to New Jersey!"
My higher power decided
I needed some humility,
so there I was
in the garbage State,
scooped up off the streets
by a born again,
clean and sober friend,
holed up in his one-bedroom,
kicking...

on the couch.
Dragging my
shot-the-fuck-out
dope-sick carcass
to daily N.A. meetings.
Everyone laughed at me
when I indentified myself
as a "heroin addict".
Come to find out,
a drug is a drug is a drug...
Nyquil or crystal,
whatever makes your life
"unmanageable".
(What a nice way to describe the long way down,
losing every single thing that I ever cared for
from my music to my family to my animals.
And of course any last shred of love.)
Come to find out,
I wasn't special.
Just another guy wrestling
putrid junkie genes.
I named my disease "Frank".
Frank did push-ups in the corner;
he drooled...
He looked me in the eye
and explained to me again
why I wasn't worth it.

BLIND FAITH AND THE DRUG ADDICT ANGEL

After three months of
walking around dead, again,
I got a call for an audition in Manhattan.
I wasn't ready yet.
The Empire State Building
looked like a giant syringe to me.
It even looked clogged,
because it had that little red light at the top.
I decided I'd hit a meeting
to lay a foundation for the trip,
so I'd get back to Jersey clean.
Called my old bass player;
she was doing great in AA.
Decided to go to a meeting with her
on 14th Street in the morning.
It was a speaker meeting.
The guy was so on.
I knew he had really been through it.
Religion...

Psychology...
None of it works.
It's the theraputic value
of one addict helping another;
that's your tiny little shot in the dark,
your microscopic pinhole
through which a fraction of us,
sometimes, gets well.
Of course the studio was right in
my old dope neighborhood.

The surrounding air:
honey heroin fog.
But I made it inside...
Jammed for about an hour;
they needed some time
to make me a tape.
Out on the street again,
a few months clean,
trembling.
Butterflies...
Roaring anguish
in my head and toes.
He walked up to me,
arms outstretched,
gave me a big hug.
A dope fiend named Donnie:
"How are you doing?" he sighed,
nodding and scratching.
"I'm good, Donnie;
I'm not shooting dope anymore."

"That's too bad," he winked,
"there's some smack around the corner."
A guy I know actually died last weekend.
A tidal wave of "fuck it" poured over me.
Whenever heroin killed someone

everyone flocked to get that particular brand.
"Lets go!" Frank said.
And then...
In New York City...

Out of hundreds and hundreds
of thousands
of people...
Who should walk by me?
The speaker from the morning meeting.
"Hey! Who are you? I'm David.
I heard you speak this morning.
I'm in a bad situation."
"Come with me right now."
I followed him into a coffee shop;
I sat there, breathing, while he talked.
"Let's get you out of here;
you got no business here anymore."
A blind man doesn't go to the movies...
Back on the train to New Jersey
there was sun and warmth
and calm.
Fred had gone to the bar car.
I thought about
how useless
Blind Faith was:
a drug addict angel
had just handed me
instant proof.

David Rat

SOCIALIZATION PROCESS

I wonder what they think of me
on this mountain of trash,
burning poems, and pearls,
and staring into the sun.

David Rat

SARA

I reach for you in the night and it takes me a moment to
realize you are not here.
These are the worst moments of my life.
You are a yardstick by which I measure my worth.

Your image of me is what I desperately wish I could be.

I wonder if I'll ever get there.
If anything ever happened to you or to James I couldn't
live.
I couldn't breathe, I couldn't go on.
The sheer terror deep in my core
is indescribable.
I live with this terror every moment
of every day.
You are so much a part of me that
sometimes I feel myself disappearing,
withering away.
I don't know who I was before you.
You are in everything I do,
everything I say,

think,
dream.
When the snow glitters in the sun
it's your breath on my neck.
The shadows are my arms around your knees,
the ravens are your eyes,
watching,
waiting.
How did we come to this?
Why are you so far away?
It seems so unfair
after we fought so hard.

Please don't let me fade away,
the part of you that is me
is all I have left.

I just want to be good;
I just want to be good;
I just want to be something...
worthy.

DAD

Dad, you were right.
My dreams were silly,
my dreams were trash.
I am paying the price -
there is a price to be
paid for dreaming...

All I want is my arms around my little boy,
his head against my chest;
instead I threw it away,
worthless junkie that I am.

Dad, you were right;
nothing else matters.
Art seems useless,
and rock and roll is only
howling at the moon.

And you're gone;
and she's gone;
and he's so faraway...

David Rat

He doesn't even
know who I am.

And Dad...
Now I'm gone.

But someday, Dad,
I will shove this dirty needle
so deep into my heart that
you will have to love me.

BORN TO USE

The third orderly hovered over me,
sticking my hand
over and over,
trying to get a hit.
"Want me to do it?" I sneered (to myself).
Every cell in my brain screamed your name.

Sara!

"What's this?" he asked
as he gently ran his finger
over the collapsed vein.

"That's old, bro."
"Your chart says you're a writer.
What do you write about?"

"Sex, drugs, rock and roll
and my dead friends..."

"Anything published?"

"Signed to a small Art House Press in Australia."
(Might as well be the moon, I thought to myself.)
And the I.V. was in.

THE DILAUDID DELUGE TRICKLED CRIPPLED CARNIVAL SPLENDOR

My first fix in three years...
"I'm administering this real slow,
so as not to burn your veins."
Dilaudid was my favorite,
better than smack.
The rush hits your head
and travels all the way to your knees.
700 miles in 7 seconds!

Jesus wept.

"Do you have a ride home?"
"Sure," I lied.
"Sending me home with something for pain?"
"Oh yeah!"

Somehow, I made it home alive.
The telephone greeted me at the door.
My little brother: "Dad's Dead"

He seemed happy
to be the one
to tell me.
I was high as fuck
but still felt like I was
punched in the stomach
as I hung up.

He was gone.
I had been such a disappointment to him.
Strong and silently principled,
the last thing he wanted
was some rock and roll
junkie poet for a son.

I looked at the bottle of Dilaudid in my hand.
Where the fuck could I get a gimmick
in this hillbilly heroin town?
I drove the Bronco to the tractor supply.
"Do you have syringes for animals?"
"What size?"
"Smallest, please?"
"22cc ok?"
(fucking horse needle)
"Sure," I drooled.

I drove home as fast as I could,
cooked those little white pills
into crystal clear oblivion,
slammed that huge needle
into my hand.

Got a hit first try.

My father sighed,
and I saw you, Sara.

I saw our little boy's smile,
    fading into black.

David Rat

JAMES, IF I SHOULD STUMBLE...
JAMES, IF I SHOULD FALL...

Before you were born, James,
I was very sick.
I was very empty inside.
Someone hurt me when I was a little boy,
and it made me feel worthless,
so I hurt myself for years and years,
hating myself.

Taking medicine so I didn't have to feel anything...
I didn't know what love was;
I thought I did.

But when you were born
everything became clear,
and I saw beauty for the first time.

I saw you, James.

They put you in my arms,

and the empty hole inside me
went from black to pure light.

And I finally understood everything
I had been searching for all my life -
all my life, James!

I finally understood what real love is!

You made me feel strong,
and I even felt like I could love myself.

If something as beautiful as you
had come in part from me,
I must be worth something...?

So I'm begging you:
Please don't give up on me, James?

It hurts...so bad!
I am so empty - again.
It aches and aches;
it never goes away.

Never!

I'm so sorry I lost my way;
not all little boys get the best daddies.

You got me;
I'm sorry.

I want to give up;
I'm tired of hurting.

I'm tired...

Happy Ending

I try not to think of you sometimes;
for this I am so ashamed.

I have to live
even though I don't want to anymore.
I have to live,
because of you.

I still have dreams,
and a little bit of hope.

I have done amazing things,
impossible things,
in my life.

I can be a good daddy,
I just know that I can,
if you want me.

I am not taking the bad medicine anymore.

I am a cowboy now!
I write poetry in the desert.
My skin is turning brown
and I feed birds from my hand.

I am trying so hard -
don't give up on me, James.

Keep me in your heart,
safe in your heart.
I will hold you
in my arms again.

or...

JAMES, IF I SHOULD FALL....

My dream for you is to be a good man,
to be kind and compassionate
and always stand up for what's right.

James, do what I could not do;
make the world a better place.

Always be kind to and protect animals;
they are the only link to magic left in the world.
In many ways animals are better than people.
I know you understand;
I saw it in your eyes.

James,
a good man cares for women;
a good man cares for children;
a good man cares for animals;
a good man cares for himself.

He cares for himself
because others depend on him.

Be kind to people less fortunate;
do your best to help ease their suffering.

Listen to your mother;
she is smart, like you.
She will know what to do.
You must never be unkind to her,
you must always protect her.
I'm counting on you.

Always try to do
"the next right thing"
whatever that may be.

Listen to your heart;
you will know.

It is that simple.

No matter what, I will always be proud of you.

I spend a lot of time wondering what kind of man you will
become.
Ultimately, you will be what you will be.
But consider the things I'm telling you now to be
important.

And the most important thing:
do not be like me.
Do not walk the path I chose.

If you have a song in your head, sing it;
if you have poetry in your soul, write it down;
if there is music in your heart, play it!

Do not succumb to self destruction:
defeat your demons .
You have to fight to be happy.
James, you have to fight!

Hold your head high!
Smile at strangers.
Be happy.
Spread happiness, James.
Spreading happiness is how we change the world.
Happy people don't hate and kill one another.

James,
if you miss me,
look for me under

the soles of your shoes.

I am everywhere, James.
I am everywhere!
Now I am a bird;
now a sunset.
Every star you see
is me smiling at you.

My heart beats inside you;
take care of my heart, son.
Take care of yourself.

James, do what I could not.

Made in the USA
Charleston, SC
12 November 2012